To Tracey,

It's so wonderful
knowing that there
wonderful people
like you around when
I am far away from
home. Let me know
when you finish your
book!

God Bless)
Sarah
Ruis
7/6/07

Timeless Treasures

Reflections of God's Word in the Wisdom of Booker T. Washington

Writings, quotations, and scriptures compiled and arranged
by two of the great-granddaughters of Booker T. Washington

Gloria Yvonne Jackson
and Sarah O'Neal Rush

Bloomington, IN Milton Keynes, UK

AuthorHouse™
1663 Liberty Drive, Suite 200
Bloomington, IN 47403
www.authorhouse.com
Phone: 1-800-839-8640

AuthorHouse™ UK Ltd.
500 Avebury Boulevard
Central Milton Keynes, MK9 2BE
www.authorhouse.co.uk
Phone: 08001974150

First published by AuthorHouse 5/17/2006

ISBN: 1-4259-2241-4 (sc)
ISBN: 1-4259-2242-2 (dj)

Printed in the United States of America
Bloomington, Indiana

This book is printed on acid-free paper.

A Gift For:_____

From:_____

"The thing to do when one feels sure that he has said or done the right thing, and is condemned, is to stand still and keep quiet. If he is right, time will show it."

(Booker T. Washington, Up From Slavery, published in 1901)

You will not need to fight in this battle. Position yourselves, stand still and see the salvation of the LORD, who is with you...

II Chronicles 20:17

Gratitude

Before I formed you in the womb, I knew you, before you were born I set you apart. I appointed you as a prophet to the nations.

Jeremiah 1:5

Above all we give thanks and glory to God, who is the savior of our souls and the Lord of our lives. We are grateful and honored to have been deliberately born into the bloodline of Booker T. Washington, which has blessed us with such a rich and inspiring heritage. We pray that God will assist us in giving Him glory as we share with others out of the extraordinary heritage with which He has blessed us.

To our devoted fathers, the late James Lyle O'Neal, Sr. and the late Theodore L. Jackson, M.D.; and to our mothers, the late Agnes Louise Washington O'Neal and Gloria Washington Jackson Baskin, two extraordinary women who are sisters and also dear friends, we dedicate this cherished volume. First, we simply thank you for giving us life. We also thank you for sacrificially giving so much of your lives in order that we would be equipped to live rich, full, and productive lives. We honor you for exemplifying the principles of our great-grandfather, in so many ways. Thank you for instilling those same principles in us, and we pray that we will in turn instill them in others.

We honor and thank our aunt, Margaret Washington Clifford, for sharing with us her exceptional knowledge about Booker T. Washington and for her tireless efforts on behalf of making certain that the life and legacy of Booker T. Washington remain vibrant and alive. We also thank her for her delicious "Washington Candies" that we have all so enjoyed over the years.

We honor and thank our late aunt, Edith Washington Johnson, who also diligently labored to keep the family history and legacy in the forefront of the collective family memory and in the memory of the public. We deeply miss you.

To our brothers and sisters, cousins and extended family, it is a blessing to share this extraordinary legacy with you.

We ask God's blessing on the life of each person who reads this book.

Acknowledgments

We would like to thank and acknowledge all of those individuals and organizations that have kept Booker T. Washington's legacy alive and who have honored his memory for so many years. To name but a few, we cite Dr. Benjamin F. Payton, president of Tuskegee University; all of the students past and present who have attended Tuskegee University; and the many Tuskegee alumni associations that are in existence across the nation. We thank those grassroots organizations that have made it their focus to model Booker T. Washington and his uplifting philosophy in their attempt to enrich, encourage, and uplift the lives of the youth and young adults of our country.

We acknowledge Lee Walker, whose New Coalition organization has championed the philosophy of Booker T. Washington for more years than we can remember, and who is such a strong advocate for the application of the philosophies of Booker T. Washington. We acknowledge Elizabeth Wright, who frequently honors Booker T. Washington and his work in her thought-provoking publication *Issues & Views*. We acknowledge Pastor Stephen Mansfield for illuminating the deep Christian faith of Booker T. Washington in his book *Then Darkness Fled*. We acknowledge Thelma Jackson Abidally, who through diligent and steadfast effort located a home in Fort Salonga, New York, that was once owned by Booker T. Washington. She was successful in having the home declared a historic landmark. We acknowledge and thank Cheryl and Hardy Brown, owners and editors of the *Black Voice News*, who have brought the history of Booker T. Washington to the Inland Empire in California in such a significant way. We acknowledge William Craft, who opened up the personal papers of Booker T. Washington in his compilation entitled *The Booker T. Washington Chronicles*, and in so doing did much to dispel the myths and revised history surrounding Booker T. Washington's memory.

In addition, we acknowledge all of those individuals and groups that are holding various events across the nation to celebrate the 150th birthday of Booker T. Washington.

Last but not least, we honor and thank our pastors, who have been so instrumental in guiding us from spiritual infancy to greater and greater spiritual maturity. We thank them for the example of their own lives as they aspire to walk not after the flesh but after the spirit. Moreover, we thank them for always lifting the name of Jesus and pointing the way to living life in the Kingdom of God. Gloria is a longtime member of West Angeles Church of God in Christ, in Los Angeles, California, pastored by the esteemed Bishop Charles E. Blake, Sr., and likewise, Sarah is a longtime member of Allen Temple, in Oakland, California, pastored by the esteemed Dr. J. Alfred Smith, Sr.

Table of Contents

# His Point of View

"From any point of view, I had rather be what I am, a member of the Negro race, than be able to claim membership with the most favoured of any other race. I have always been made sad when I have heard members of any race claiming rights and privileges, or certain badges of distinction, on the ground simply that they were members of this or that race, regardless of their own individual worth or attainments. I have been made to feel sad for such persons because I am conscious of the fact that mere connection with what is known as a superior race will not permanently carry an individual forward unless he has individual worth, and mere connection with what is regarded as an inferior race will not finally hold an individual back if he possesses intrinsic, individual merit. Every persecuted individual and race should get much consolation out of the great human law, which is universal and eternal, that merit, no matter under what skin found, is, in the long run, recognized and rewarded. This I have said here, not to call attention to myself as an individual, but to the race to which I am proud to belong."

(Booker T. Washington, Up From Slavery, published in 1901)

Introduction

Believing that the wisdom of Booker T. Washington, one of the greatest leaders of the Black race in the history of the United States, is as relevant today as it was when it was first spoken, we have lovingly compiled some of our favorite of his cherished quotations.

Not many have heard the story of how the young slave boy Booker became Booker "T." Washington. The T stands for Taliaferro, a name his mother had given him at his birth and a name some say might indicate the identity of his biological father.

"Washington" was merely a name that young Booker uttered at the first school he attended. It was the first name of his stepfather, Washington Ferguson, which is perhaps the reason this name came to his mind as the roll was being called one morning. He realized that most of the students answered to two names and he had only one. When he was called upon he simply added Washington and answered Booker Washington; thus, Washington became his last name.

As two of the great-granddaughters of Booker T. Washington, we have our own version of the significance of the T in his name. We affectionately like to say that the T actually stands for the *Timeless Treasures* hidden in the wisdom of our great-grandfather's words; hence, the title of our book.

But for a change to account for the vernacular of the day (i.e., Negro or colored to African-American or black), the liberating wisdom of Booker T. Washington's words is as relevant and necessary today as it was in his lifetime. We feel we would be remiss if we did not add that the wisdom that he proclaimed is not only relevant to the black American race, but it is also relevant to any race or nationality whose goal is to strive to achieve excellence in every area of life.

Knowing that our great-grandfather relied upon his deep and abiding faith and trust in God to guide him, we have included, besides his words, some of our favorite scriptures from "The Word," the Bible.

The evidence of God in his life was striking. Though he was born into a system of chattel slavery, in his brief lifetime of only fifty-nine years he rose to become one of the most captivating orators and spokespersons of his time and the leader of over ten million of his race. He was the consummate statesman and diplomat, a famous educator, and the founder and builder of Tuskegee Institute and the National Negro Business League. He was also a builder of men and of women.

Booker T. Washington was an advisor to presidents McKinley, Roosevelt, and Taft; was received by the king of Denmark; and enjoyed tea with the queen of England at Buckingham Palace. He was the first black American to be commemorated on United States coins and postage stamps, and to have a U.S. Navy vessel named in his honor. He was the first black American to have his birthplace declared a national monument.

Tuskegee and the National Negro Business League became training grounds for free-market access. Entrepreneurial skills were refined and multitudes of trained blacks started thriving businesses. These businesses provided jobs and became the backdrop of flourishing communities that served as anchors for our race as we pushed forward toward economic self-sufficiency.

While most people in the United States were paying scant attention to the problems and concerns of blacks in other parts of the world, Booker T. Washington lifted his voice and used his considerable influence on their behalf as well. In 1913, amid all of his other responsibilities, he became the first black American to convene an international conference at Tuskegee Institute to address these concerns. Representatives came from Africa, the West Indies, Europe, South America, and from all over the United States.

Against the backdrop of his enormous public undertakings, it must also be remembered that he was a loving, devoted, and cherished husband and father. He was also a best-selling author. His inspiring autobiography, *Up From Slavery*, the most renowned of the many books he wrote, has never been out of print. It has been translated into over seventeen languages, and it has been an inspiration to people throughout the world. Though many, these achievements are but a brief synopsis of the manifold accomplishments and honors of this extraordinary man.

It could only have been God guiding Booker T. Washington and governing his life. Even after experiencing the harsh realities of slavery, and later watching as the hope embodied in the Reconstruction period was dismantled, he still possessed the strength of character to utter the words, "I will let no man drag me down so low as to make me hate him." He refused even to hate his former slave master, choosing instead to spend his time and energy living by the principles of the Word of God, lifting people up and appealing to what was best in them. He spent his life lighting candles in the lives of others, rather than wasting his life cursing the darkness.

W. E. B. Du Bois called Booker T. Washington a "Joshua called of God." President Theodore Roosevelt, in his summation of the life of Booker T. Washington, reflected that he nearly perfectly lived the scripture from Micah 6:8: "And what doth the Lord require of thee, than to do justly, and to love mercy, and to walk humbly with thy God?"

We offer these words of Booker T. Washington with the hope that you will revisit, or visit for the first time, his great practical wisdom. We believe that as you reflect upon his words and apply the wisdom contained therein that your life will be enriched, and in turn you will enrich the lives of those around you. It is our further hope that your faith and trust in God will be strengthened as you meditate upon the life-giving scriptures of the Word of God.

Gloria Yvonne Jackson, J.D.,
and Sarah O'Neal Rush, M.A.

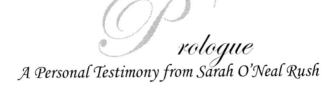

Prologue
A Personal Testimony from Sarah O'Neal Rush

As I witnessed the marvelous works of my great-grandfather during our first Booker T. Washington extended family reunion, held on the grounds of Tuskegee University in 1996, for the first time the legacy that I'd taken for granted for so many years began to come alive. Since that day, less than ten years before the time of this writing, my world has changed dramatically.

Immediately upon arriving on campus we were greeted by news reporters, journalists, faculty, and students who asked for autographs, photos, and just a chance to talk and get to know us. They were in awe that the descendants of this extraordinary man were still alive. I was in awe at how they cared so deeply, nearly eighty-one years after his death.

As I toured the campus, I was most inspired by the buildings before me that were erected under the direction of Booker T. Washington. He and other former slaves who were his students and staff built each building by hand, brick by brick, using bricks that they made. These bricks were of such high quality that contractors, business owners, and others would come from miles around to purchase them. The buildings on campus still stand today, 125 years later.

When I returned home from this reunion I passionately set out to discover all I could about the life and legacy of my great-grandfather. I read, I studied, and I asked questions. I came to realize that there was an obligation tied to the privilege of being born into this great lineage, and it was to carry on the legacy using the gifts that God bestowed up me.

With a passion for writing, a personal story of rising above circumstances, and professional training in mental health, I eventually developed the Booker T. Washington Empowerment Network, Inc. (B.T.W.E.N.), to inspire and uplift others and to revive the history, and the concepts and philosophies of my great-grandfather through writing, life coaching, and public speaking.

After our first two biennial family reunions in Tuskegee, the family decided to follow our great ancestor's footsteps on our next few reunions. In 2000 we came together in Franklin County, Virginia, where he was born into slavery, and where the plantation and a reconstructed model of his slave cabin are now national monuments. In 2002 we went to Malden, West Virginia, where he and his family lived immediately after slavery ended. In 2004 we met in Hampton, Virginia, at Hampton University, where he attained for his formal education. We will complete the journey in 2006 as we come full circle back to the campus of Tuskegee University to celebrate his 150th birthday.

In 2003 our family attended a rededication ceremony in Kings Canyon National Forest of a giant redwood tree that was initially dedicated to Colonel Charles Young, a Buffalo Soldier, who in 1903 completed extraordinary work on the roads in the forest. Rather than accept the honor, in his modesty Colonel Young asked that the tree be named for someone whom he greatly admired, Booker T. Washington.

In March of 2004 we attended the unveiling of a Booker T. Washington bust at the historic Mission Inn in Riverside, California. He spoke at the Mission Inn more than ninety years ago, one year prior to his death, as part of his campaign to raise funds for Tuskegee and other black institutions of higher learning. One of the most poignant and beautiful portions of the ceremony was the release of nine doves which represented the lives of people he touched and the nine decades that had passed since his visit there.

As I continue to learn of the virtues of my great-grandfather beyond the textbooks, incredible discoveries continue to unfold. One of the most touching is the direct tie he had to a school around the corner from where my husband, Anthony, was born and raised, Laurinburg Institute in Laurinburg, North Carolina. This school is a major landmark in this small, rural, unassuming town. On several occasions when we traveled back to my husband's boyhood home, we would pass by the school and he would share stories with me about it. Little did we know at the time that my great-grandfather had anything to do with its existence.

Eventually, in 2003 I learned that in the early 1900s, the black parents in Laurinburg wrote to Booker T. Washington to ask him to help them begin a school so their children could receive an education beyond the elementary years. Responding to their call, he sent two of his graduates from Tuskegee, Emmanuel and Tinny McDuffie, to open the school. Established in 1904 on the same principles as the Tuskegee Institute—education of the hand, head, and heart—Laurinburg Institute has outlasted dozens of other private black prep schools that were forced to close their doors after the 1954 *Brown vs. Board of Education* ruling. Today it is one of the only four private black prep schools in the country.

In 2004, in Laurinburg, North Carolina, I had the privilege of being the keynote speaker for one of their many centennial celebration events.

At home, in Northern California, in the summer of 2004, as the day drew near for a book signing, where I was to autograph copies of my great-grandfather's autobiography, Up From Slavery, I began to feel uneasy because of an unexpected turn of events leading up to the occasion. As my anxiety increased, my husband and I made a rare request to meet with our pastor, Dr. J. Alfred Smith, Sr. Ours is a large congregation and the burdens on our pastor often can be great, so I hesitated to add something else to his plate, but the heaviness was beginning to take its toll on me.

When my husband and I first sat down in our pastor's study, I showed him some of my family memorabilia, including an original copy of Up From Slavery, autographed by my grandfather, Ernest Davidson Washington. He opened another book that I brought, compiled by my grandfather, on the wisdom of Booker T. Washington. As he began reading aloud from it, it brought tears of joy to his eyes. As he continued turning the pages, encouragingly he said, "This is history, this is history, this is important." He later read from the Bible, Jeremiah 1:5, "Before you were born I knew you, and then he prayed with us. When we left his office, I realized that we never really discussed the upcoming book signing, yet I left feeling inspired. The book signing event turned out to be a wonderful occasion.

Ironically, in the sanctuary of my church, Allen Temple, there are several beautifully crafted stained-glass windows that adorn the walls directly above the pews where I usually sit on Sunday. These windows house a magnificent collection of pictures of great black Americans within each window frame. When I look up to see Booker T. Washington among them, I am constantly reminded of the blessing that God has bestowed upon my life.

As I continue to carry on this legacy, I continue to meet so many wonderful people along the way, of all colors, from all walks of life, who come up to me to share stories of how Booker T. Washington has touched, influenced, and inspired their lives, or to simply give me yet another important piece of his history.

The journey has only begun for me, and only God knows where it will go from here.

Sarah O'Neal Rush

The Content of Our Character

Strong moral and ethical character is not made up of the circles that we travel in, the color of our skin, or the size of our wallet; it is when we do the right thing, not only when people are watching, but also when no one else is around. Thus, character is made up of what is truly in our hearts.

If we begin making conscious efforts to instill strong moral and ethical character in children when they are very young, the future will be brighter because we will produce better adults. This is the real foundation of good character and successful living.

Sarah

Only take heed, and guard your life diligently, lest you forget the things which your eyes have seen and lest they depart from your [mind and] heart all the days of your life. Teach them to your children and your children's children.

Deuteronomy 4:9

The Content of Our Character

Quotations from Booker T. Washington

Character is power. If you want to be powerful in the world, if you want to be strong, influential and useful, you can be so in no better way than by having a strong character.

Blessed is the man

> *Who walks not in the counsel of the ungodly,*
> *Nor stands in the path of sinners,*
> *Nor sits in the seat of the scornful;*

> *But his delight is in the law of the Lord,*
> *And in His law he meditates day and night.*

> *He shall be like a tree*
> *Planted by the rivers of water,*
> *That brings forth its fruit in its season,*
> *Whose leaf also shall not wither;*
> *And whatever he does shall prosper.*

Psalm 1:1-3

Let us hold up our head, and with firm and steady tread go manfully forward. No one likes to feel that he is continually following a funeral procession.

Do not grieve, for the joy of the Lord is your strength.

Nehemiah 8:10

We shall prosper in proportion as we learn to draw the line between the superficial and the substantial, the ornamental gewgaws of life and the useful.

Beloved, I wish above all things that thou mayest prosper and be in health, even as thy soul prospereth.

III John 1:2

When measured by the standard of eternal, or even present justice that race is greatest that has learned to exhibit the greatest patience, the greatest self-control, the greatest forbearance, the greatest interest in the poor, in the unfortunate—that has been able to live up in a high and pure atmosphere, and to dwell above hatred and acts of cruelty. He who would become greatest among us must become the least.

But many who are first will be last, and the last first.

Mark 10:31

The average individual thinks he knows a great deal more than he does know. The individual who really knows more than he thinks he knows, is rare indeed.

For I say, through the grace given unto me, to every man that is among you, not to think of himself more highly than he ought to think; but to think soberly, according as God hath dealt to every man the measure of faith.

Romans 12:3

It is the weak individual, as a rule, who is constantly calling attention to the other side—to the dark and discouraging things of life.

Death and life are in the power of the tongue.

Proverbs 18:21

It requires little wisdom or statesmanship to repress, to crush out, to retard the hopes and aspirations of a people; but the highest and most profound statesmanship is shown in guiding and stimulating a people so that every fiber of body, mind, and soul shall be made to contribute in the highest degree to the usefulness of the state.

As each one has received a special gift, employ it in serving one another as good stewards of the manifold grace of God. Whoever speaks, is to do so as one who is speaking the utterances of God; whoever serves is to do so as one who is serving by the strength which God supplies; so that in all things God may be glorified through Jesus Christ, to whom belongs the glory and dominion forever and ever. Amen.

I Peter 4:10-11

It must be remembered that no individual of any race can contribute to the solution of any general problem until he has first worked out his own peculiar problem.

First, remove the plank from your own eye, and then you will see clearly to remove the speck from your brother's eye.

Matthew 7:5

The deeds which uplift or degrade human character measure the life of a nation.

If a kingdom is divided against itself, that kingdom cannot stand. And if a house is divided against itself, that house cannot stand.

Mark 3:24-25

It often requires more courage to suffer in silence than to rebel, more courage not to strike back than to retaliate, more courage to be silent than to speak.

Blessed are the meek, for they shall inherit the earth.

Matthew 5:5

There is no wealth in the mines or in the seas equal to that which is created by the growth and establishment in a people of habits of thrift and intelligent forethought.

Wealth obtained by fraud dwindles, but the one who gathers by labor increases it.

Proverbs 13:11

We should not be discouraged as a race. No man discouraged ever wins a victory.

And Jesus said unto him, no man, having put his hand to the plough, and looking back, is fit for the Kingdom of God.

Luke 9:62

In nine cases out of ten, the person who cultivates the habit of looking on the dark side of life is the little person, the miserable person, the one who is weak in heart, mind and purpose—on the other hand, the person who cultivates the habit of looking on the bright side of life, and who calls attention to the beautiful and encouraging things in life, is, in nine cases out of ten, the strong individual, the one to whom the world goes for intelligent advice and support.

Finally, brethren, whatsoever things are true, whatsoever things are honest, whatsoever things are just, whatsoever things are pure, whatsoever things are lovely, whatsoever things are of a good report, if there be any virtue, and if there be any praise, think on these things.

Philippians 4:8

There are too many people in the world who give their whole lives grasping at the shadow instead of the substance.

For where your treasure is, there will your heart be also.

Matthew 6:21

The individual who puts the most into life is the one who gets the most out of life.

> *Abide in Me, and I in you. As the branch cannot bear fruit of itself unless it abides in the vine, so neither can you unless you abide in Me. I am the vine, you are the branches; he who abides in Me and I in him, he bears much fruit, for apart from Me you can do nothing.*
>
> *John 15:4-5*

It is the wise individual who makes up his mind that life is not going to be all sunshine, that all is not going to be perpetual pleasure.

> *Those who sow in tears shall reap in joy.*
>
> *Psalm 126:5*

The more important things are those which are hidden; the least important are those which can be seen.

> *For man looks at the outward appearance, but the Lord looks at the heart.*
>
> *I Samuel 16:7*

It is with an ignorant race as it is with a child; it craves at first the superficial, the ornamental, the signs of progress rather than the reality. The foundation of progress for blacks must be in truth and not in pretense.

When I was a child, I talked like a child, I thought like a child, I reasoned like a child. When I became a man, I put childish ways behind me.

I Corinthians 13:11

We should know our weaknesses as well as our strengths if we would attain to the best in our civilization.

Therefore humble yourselves under the mighty hand of God, that He may exalt you in due time, casting all your care upon Him, for He cares for you.

I Peter 5:6-7

I have long since ceased to cherish any spirit of bitterness against the Southern white people on account of the enslavement of my race.

And when you stand praying, forgive, if you have aught against any: that your Father also which is in heaven may forgive you your trespasses. But if ye do not forgive, neither will your Father which is in heaven forgive your trespasses.

Mark 11:25-26

A nation cannot teach its youths to think in terms of destruction and oppression without brutalizing and blunting the tender conscience and sense of justice of the youths of that country.

The thief cometh not, but for to steal, and to kill, and to destroy: I am come that they might have life, and that they might have it more abundantly.

John 10:10

If the Negro race wishes to grow strong, it must learn to respect itself, not to be ashamed. It must learn that it will only grow in proportion as its members have confidence in it, in proportion as they believe that it is a coming race.

If thou canst believe, all things are possible to him that believeth.

Mark 9:23

Through the church we must teach our young people they must not mistake the signs of civilization for civilization itself, must teach the young men that cheap, flashy clothing do not make the man; that it is better to be clad in rags or homespun and have real character, real worth, and have some land and a bank account and some education back of it, than to weave the most gaudy and flashy clothing with nothing back of those clothes. In the cities in many cases, the temptation is to get a dress suit before we get a bank account. There is the problem of the loafer which is becoming extremely difficult in all our large cities, which the church must concern itself with.

Therefore I tell you, do not worry about your life, what you will eat or drink; or about your body, what you will wear. Is not life more important than food, and the body more important than clothes? Look at the birds of the air; they do not sow or reap or store away in barns, and yet your heavenly Father feeds them. Are you not much more valuable than they? Who of you by worrying can add a single hour to his life? And why do you worry about your clothes?

Matthew 6:25-28

One of the greatest temptations young people have, who live on the lower side of life, is to engage in profane, vulgar, and boisterous conversation. The nature of a person's conversation largely determines what he is. Young people especially should seek to converse with persons whose conversation, whose thought, is pure and refined. The influence of unhealthy conversation is so great that nothing can counter the harm it does a person's character. If a young person finds himself associated with a person of either sex who has no regard for healthy thinking and pure expression, he should rid himself of the association. If he does not do so, he will eventually fall to the level of his companion. It is true that "birds of a feather flock together."

Do not let any unwholesome talk come out of your mouths, but only what is helpful for building others up according to their needs, that it may benefit those who listen.

Ephesians 4:29

He who lives outside the law is a slave. The free man is the man who lives within the law, whether that law be the physical or the divine.

Where there is no vision, the people perish: but he that keepeth the law, happy is he.

Proverbs 29:18

The persons who live constantly in a fault-finding atmosphere, who see only the dark side of life, become negative characters. They are the people who never go forward.

A good man out of the good treasure of his heart bringeth forth that which is good; and an evil man out of the evil treasure of his heart bringeth forth that which is evil: for of the abundance of his heart his mouth speaketh.

Luke 6:45

If others would be little, we can be great; if others would be mean, we can be good. If others would push us down, we can help push them up.

Instead of their shame My people will receive a double portion, and instead of disgrace they will rejoice in their inheritance; and so they will inherit a double portion in their land, and everlasting joy will be theirs.

Isaiah 61:7

Character, not circumstances, makes the man.

And not only that, but we also glory in tribulations; knowing that tribulation produces perseverance; and perseverance, character; and character, hope.

Romans 5:3-4

I sometimes fear that we yield to the temptation of parading and advertising our difficulties too much before the public. I sometimes fear that we are prone to advertise our disadvantages rather than our advantages.

Wherefore, my beloved brethren, let every man be swift to hear, slow to speak, slow to wrath: For the wrath of man worketh not the righteousness of God.

James 1:19-20

Opportunities never come a second time, nor do they abide our leisure. The years come but once, and swiftly pass on, bearing the ineffaceable record we put upon them. If we make them beautiful years, we must do it moment by moment as they glide before us.

Therefore we do not lose heart. Though outwardly we are wasting away, yet inwardly we are being renewed day by day. For our light and momentary troubles are achieving for us an eternal glory that far outweighs them all.

II Corinthians 4:16-17

Exalt Excellence

Largely because of the efforts of Booker T. Washington, Tuskegee Institute and its progeny, at the turn of the 20th century, black students were routinely winning oratory and literary contests against white students from far better funded schools.

Illiteracy among blacks was rapidly becoming a condition of the past. Many of the students hailed from small southern shanty schools, but they achieved, nonetheless, because they expected to achieve. They had been taught to revere excellence.

We must remind ourselves, and continually inform our youth, of our remarkable past. It is a dishonor to our inspired history to allow some of our young people to adopt attitudes that to be smart or to aspire to excellence is somehow "selling out" or "acting white." So many before us sacrificed greatly so that we would have the opportunity to excel.

Our history is replete with examples of those, who like Booker T. Washington, lived lives of significance and contributed greatly toward elevating others because they adopted principles of discipline, hard work, and excellence. They passed this work ethic and standard of excellence on to their children. We must now continue in that vein and lift up excellence as a standard as we apply our best efforts to achieve our best result.

Gloria

Then this Daniel was preferred above the presidents and princes, because an excellent spirit was in him; And the king thought to set him over the whole realm.

Daniel 6:3

Exalt Excellence

Quotations from Booker T. Washington

I believe that any man's life will be filled with constant, unexpected encouragements if he makes up his mind to do his level best each day of his life—that is, tries to make each day as nearly as possible the highest mark of pure, unselfish, useful living.

Who is wise and understanding among you? Let him show it by his good life, by deeds done in the humility that comes from wisdom.

James 3:13

Too often the educational value of doing well what is done, however little, is overlooked. One thing well done prepares the mind to do the next thing better. Not how much, but how well, should be the motto. One problem thoroughly understood is of more value than a score poorly mastered.

A good man obtains favor from the Lord, but the Lord condemns a crafty man.

Proverbs 12:2

One should learn to do the common things in an uncommon way.

Whatever you do, do your work heartily as for the Lord rather than for men, knowing that from the Lord you will receive the reward of the inheritance. It is the Lord Christ whom you serve.

Colossians 3:23-24

Every man and every woman who is worthy to be respected and praised and recognized will be respected and praised and recognized.

Now we ask you, brothers, to respect those who work hard among you, who are over you in the Lord and who admonish you. Hold them in the highest regard in love because of their work. Live in peace with each other.

I Thessalonians 5:12-13

Happily the world has at last reached the point where it no longer feels that in order for a person to be a great scholar he has got to read a number of text books, that he has got to master a certain number of foreign languages, but the world has come to the conclusion that the person who has learned to use his mind whether it has come about through the use of a tool or through the use of any other implement— that person who has mastered something, who understands what he is doing, who is master of himself in the classroom, out in the world, master of himself everywhere, that person is a scholar.

And every man that striveth for the mastery is temperate in all things. Now they do it to obtain a corruptible crown, but we an incorruptible.

I Corinthians 9:25

If you get into the habit of putting in hard and conscientious work, doing a little duty well, no matter how insignificant, if you get into the habit of doing well whatever falls to your hands, whether in the light or in the dark—you will find that you are going to lay a foundation for success.

> *Whoever comes to Me, and hears My sayings and does them, I will show you whom he is like: He is like a man building a house, who dug deep and laid the foundation on the rock. And when the flood arose, the stream beat vehemently against that house, and could not shake it, for it was founded on the rock. But he who heard and did nothing is like a man who built a house on the earth without a foundation against which the stream beat vehemently; and immediately it fell. And the ruin of that house was great.*
>
> *Luke 6:47-49*

Let every Negro strive to become the most useful and indispensable man in his community. A useless, shiftless, idle class is a menace and a danger to any community. When an individual produces what the world wants, whether it is a product of hand, head, heart, the world does not long stop to inquire what is the color of the skin of the producer.

> *And we urge you, brothers, warn those who are idle, encourage the timid, help the weak, be patient with everyone. Make sure that nobody pays back wrong for wrong, but always try to be kind to each other and to everyone else.*
>
> *I Thessalonians 5:14-15*

Civilization demands from every individual the very utmost that the Creator has placed at his command.

> *And God blessed them and said to them, "Be fruitful, multiply, and fill the earth, and subdue it [using all its vast resources in the service of God and man]; and have dominion over the fish of the sea, the birds of the air, and over every living creature that moves upon the earth."*
>
> *Genesis 1:28*

The race, like the individual, that makes itself indispensable has solved most of its problems.

> *Well done, thy good and faithful servant: thou hast been faithful over a few things, I will make thee ruler over many things: enter into the joy of the Lord.*
>
> *Matthew 25:21*

Show me a person who merely does as a duty what he is asked to do, and I will show you a person who is never in constant demand—a person who is not going to be very valuable to humanity.

> *He repays a man for what he has done; he brings upon him what his conduct deserves.*
>
> *Job 34:11*

Few things help an individual more than to place responsibility upon him, and to let him know that you trust him.

Trust in the Lord with all thine heart; and lean not unto thine own understanding. In all thy ways acknowledge Him, and He shall direct thy paths.

Proverbs 3:5-6

You cannot afford to do a thing poorly. You are more injured in shirking your work or half doing a job than the person for whom you are working.

Now this I say, he who sows sparingly shall also reap sparingly, and he who sows bountifully shall also reap bountifully.

II Corinthians 9:6

The man who has learned to do something better than anyone else, has learned to do a common thing in an uncommon manner, is the man who has a power and influence that no adverse circumstances can take from him.

Not slothful in business; fervent in spirit; serving the Lord.

Romans 12:11

Education of The Head, The Hand, and The Heart

Only sixteen years after slavery ended, in 1881 Tuskegee University was founded and modeled after the same principles as Hampton University—educating the head, the hand, and the heart.

The "head" through strong academic class work, the "hand" through manual labor, and vocational training, and the "heart" through an emphasis on service, selflessness and Christianity.

Today, in this 21st century, while there are many more opportunities in the area of the hand, it is the head and the heart which must remain constant, as we continue to realize, and contribute to, the unfolding of a better world.

Sarah

For wisdom will enter your heart, and knowledge will be pleasant to your soul.

Proverbs 2:10

Education of The Head, The Hand, and The Heart

Quotations from Booker T. Washington

The end of all good education, whether of head or heart, is to make an individual good, to make him useful, to make him powerful; is to give him goodness, usefulness and power in order that he may exert a helpful influence upon his fellows.

For everyone to whom much is given of him much shall be required.

Luke 12:48

A person is never educated until he is able to go into the swamps and woods and see something that is beautiful in the trees and shrubs there; is able to see something beautiful in the grass and flowers that surround him, in short, to see something beautiful, elevating, in everything that God has created.

The earth is the Lord's, and all its fullness, the world and those who dwell therein.

Psalm 24:1

That education, whether of black men or white men, that gives one physical courage to stand in front of a cannon and fails to give him moral courage to stand up in defense of right and justice, is a failure.

For the weapons of our warfare are not carnal but mighty through God to the pulling down of strong holds; casting down imaginations and every high thing that exalteth itself against the knowledge of God, and bringing into captivity every thought to the obedience to Christ.

II Corinthians 10:4-5

One of the weakest points in connection with the present development of the race is that so many get the idea that the mere filling of the head with a knowledge of mathematics, the sciences, and literature means success in life.

A wise man will hear, and increase learning; and a man of understanding shall attain unto wise counsels.

Proverbs 1:5

The study of art that does not result in making the strong less willing to oppress the weak means little.

He who oppresses the poor shows contempt for their Maker, but whoever is kind to the needy honors God.

Proverbs 14:31

There is no permanent safety for any of us or for our institutions except in the enlightenment of the whole people, except in continuing to educate until people everywhere be too big to be little, too broad to be narrow, be too high to stoop to littleness and meanness.

Do not be overcome by evil, but overcome evil with good.

Romans 12:21

The Negro should have the most thorough mental and religious training; for without it no race can succeed.

Study to show thyself approved unto God, a workman that needeth not to be ashamed, rightly dividing the word of truth.

II Timothy 2:15

Ignorance is more costly to any state than education.

My people are destroyed for lack of knowledge.

Hosea 4:6

The want of proper direction of the use of the Negro's education results in tempting too many to live mainly by their wits, without producing anything that is of real value to the world.

It is not good to have zeal without knowledge, nor to be hasty and miss the way.

Proverbs 19:2

My experience has taught me that the surest way to success in education, and in any other line for that matter, is to stick close to the common and familiar things that concern the greater part of the people the greater part of the time.

There were no needy persons among them. For from time to time those who owned lands or houses sold them, brought the money from the sales and put it at the apostles feet, and it was distributed to anyone as he had need.

Acts 4:34-35

The world cares very little about what a man or woman knows; it is what the man or woman is able to do.

Whatever you do in word or deed, do all in the name of the Lord Jesus, giving thanks through Him to God the Father.

Colossians 3:17

It is important and right that all privileges of law be ours, but it is vastly more important that we be prepared for the exercise of these privileges.

Righteousness exalteth a nation: but sin is a reproach to any people.

Proverbs 14:34

It is not possible to improve the condition in any race until the mind is awakened and improved.

Do not be conformed to this world, but be transformed by the renewing of your mind that you may prove what is that good and acceptable and perfect will of God.

Romans 12:2

One language well learned is of more value than six of which we only have a smattering. Show me a young man who is dabbling in all subjects and mastering none, and I will show you a man who will go floundering through life without purpose, without business, without stability, without top or bottom, now here, now there, a complete and disgraceful failure everywhere.

For let not that man think that he shall receive anything of the Lord. A double minded man is unstable in all his ways.

James 1:7-8

We must not be deceived by the mere fact a person can read or write. Unless he has received that broader training which enables him to know the object of education, the uses of education; unless he receives that broader training which will make him realize that book education is useless without character, without industry, without the saving habit, without the willingness to contribute his part toward law and order and the highest and best in the community, his mere book education will in many cases mean little or nothing.

Wisdom is the principal thing: therefore get wisdom: and with all thy getting, get understanding.

Proverbs 4:7

Education may be valuable or worthless. Gold may be valuable or worthless. Gold touching the markets of the world is valuable; a bushel of gold dollars in a boat in mid-ocean lying at the feet of a hungry man is worthless. Gold has got to touch something to impart real value to it. Education has got to touch something in the same way; has got to quicken something into life to be of value.

For what shall it profit a man, if he shall gain the whole world, and lose his own soul?

Mark 8:36

Any individual who has learned to love good books, to love the best newspapers, the best magazines, and has learned to spend some portion of the day in communication with them, is a happy individual.

And this is my prayer: that your love may abound more and more in knowledge and depth of insight.

Philippians 1:9

An educated man on the street with his hands in his pockets is not one whit more benefit to society than an ignorant man on the streets with his hands in his pockets.

Lazy hands make a man poor, but diligent hands bring wealth.

Proverbs 10:4

There should be a more vital and practical connection between the Negro's educated brain and his opportunity to earn his daily living.

It is written, "man shall not live by bread alone, but by every word that proceeds from the mouth of God."

Matthew 4:4

The older I grow, the more I am convinced that there is no education which one can get from books and costly apparatus that is equal to that which can be gotten from contact with great men and women.

Where no wise guidance is the people fall, but in the multitude of counselors there is safety.

Proverbs 11:14

It seems to me that the temptation in education and missionary effort is to do for people that which was done a thousand years ago, or is being done for people a thousand miles away, without always making a careful study of the needs and conditions of the people whom we are trying to help. The temptation is to run all the people through a certain educational mould regardless of the condition of the subject or the end to be accomplished.

We have different gifts, according to the grace given to us. If a man's gift is prophesying, let him use it in proportion to his faith. If it is serving, let him serve; if it is teaching, let him teach; if it is encouraging, let him encourage; if it is contributing to the needs of others, let him give generously; if it is leadership, let him govern diligently; if it is showing mercy, let him do it cheerfully.

Romans 12:6-8

The highly educated person is the one who is considerate of those individuals who are less fortunate.

The righteous care about justice for the poor but the wicked have no such concern.

Proverbs 29:7

You may fill your heads with knowledge or skillfully train your hands, but unless it is based upon high, upright character, upon a true heart, it will amount to nothing. You will be no better than the most ignorant.

For as he thinketh in his heart, so is he.

Proverbs 23:7

How I wish from the most cultured and highly endowed university in the great North to the humblest log cabin schoolhouse in Alabama, we could burn, as it were, into the hearts and heads of all, that usefulness, that service to our brother, is the supreme end of education.

And besides this, giving all diligence, add to your faith virtue; and to virtue knowledge; and to knowledge temperance; and to temperance patience; and to patience godliness; and to godliness brotherly kindness; and to brotherly kindness charity: For if these things be in you, and abound, they make you that ye shall neither be barren nor unfruitful in the knowledge of our Lord Jesus Christ.

II Peter 1:5-8

Race Relations—
Let Freedom Ring!

Booker T. Washington believed in a united America. He, too, had a dream. He looked forward to a time when, as Dr. Martin Luther King, Jr. would express so eloquently a half-century later, all people in America would be judged not by the color of their skin, but rather by the content of their character. He was aware, however, that our people carried deep scars and pains as a result of the years of suffering under slavery. He knew that it was vital for our race to achieve something for ourselves. We had built so much of the south, but we were building on behalf of others and under coercion.

Among the many reasons the work of Booker T. Washington was so important is that through his work he taught us how to believe in ourselves and in our abilities. He demonstrated to us, and required that we demonstrate to ourselves the resourcefulness and resilience we possessed as a people, not even twenty years after the formal abolition of the institution of slavery in America.

It must be noted and celebrated that Tuskegee Normal and Industrial Institute, now University, was a wholly conceived, wholly built, and wholly administered Black American institution, of higher learning. It was the best in the land, and from its development and its success our people derived great satisfaction, great strength, and great pride.

Gloria

Now thanks be unto God which always causes us to triumph in Christ...

II Corinthians 2:14

Race Relations— Let Freedom Ring!

Quotations from Booker T. Washington

Slavery presented a problem of destruction; freedom presents one of construction.

> *Henceforth I call you not servants; for the servant knoweth not what his lord doeth: but I have called you friends; for all things that I have heard of my Father I have made known unto you.*
>
> *John 15:15*

That person is the broadest, strongest, and most useful who sees something to love and admire in all races, no matter what their color.

> *I perceive that God is no respecter of persons: But in every nation he that feareth Him and, worketh righteousness, is accepted with Him.*
>
> *Acts 10:34-35*

One cannot hold another down in the ditch without staying down in the ditch with him—and in helping the man who is down to rise, the man who is up is freeing himself from a burden that would else drag him down. For the man who is down, there is always something to hope for, always something to be gained.

But God has chosen the foolish things of the world to put to shame the wise, and God has chosen the weak things of the world to put to shame the things which are mighty; and the base things of the world and the things which are despised God has chosen, and the things which are not, to bring to nothing the things that are, that no flesh should glory in His presence.

1 Corinthians 1:27-29

To those of my race who depend upon bettering their conditions in a foreign land, or who underestimate the importance of cultivating friendly relations with the Southern white man who is their next-door neighbor, I would say: Cast down your bucket where you are. Cast it down in making friends, in every honorable way, of the people of all races by whom you are surrounded. Cast it down in agriculture, mechanics, in commerce, in domestic service, and in the professions.

Jesus said unto him, Thou shalt love the Lord thy God with all thy heart, and with all thy soul, and with all thy mind. This is the first and great commandment. And the second is like unto it, Thou shalt love thy neighbor as thyself. On these two commandments hang all the law and prophets.

Matthew 22:37-40

There is no defense or security for any of us except in the highest intelligence and development of all.

> *And He gave some, apostles; and some, prophets; and some, evangelists; and some, pastors and teachers; for the perfecting of the saints, for the work of the ministry, for the edifying of the body of Christ: Till we all come in the unity of the faith, and of the knowledge of the Son of God, unto a perfect man, unto the measure of the stature of the fullness of Christ.*
>
> *Ephesians 4:11-13*

One cannot lynch disease, ignorance, or idleness; these conditions cannot only be cured by education, but they can be helped forward immensely by the best white people and the best colored people in every community conferring frequently together concerning their mutual interests.

> *For where two or three are gathered together in My name, there am I in the midst of them.*
>
> *Matthew 18:20*

The white man who begins by cheating the Negro, ends by cheating a white man.

> *There is a way that seemeth right unto a man, but the end thereof are the ways of death.*
>
> *Proverbs 16:25*

Injustice cannot work harm upon the oppressed without injuring the oppressor.

If My people, which are called by My name, shall humble themselves, and pray, and seek My face, and turn from their wicked ways; then will I hear from heaven, and will forgive their sin, and will heal their land.

II Chronicles 7:14

I pity from the bottom of my heart any individual who is so unfortunate as to get into the habit of holding race prejudice, for nothing else makes one so blind and narrow.

When the enemy shall come in like a flood, the spirit of the Lord shall lift up a standard against him.

Isaiah 59:19

Lynchings and burnings, which are often witnessed by numbers of young and tender children, do the race that inflicts these punishments, many times more harm, by blunting its moral sense, than the race or individual against whom they are directed. Physical death comes to the one Negro lynched in a county, but death of the morals, death of the soul, come to the thousands responsible for the lynching.

"No weapon formed against you shall prosper, and every tongue which rises against you in judgment you shall condemn. This is the heritage of the servants of the Lord, and their righteousness is from Me," says the Lord.

Isaiah 54:17

I would not change my color if I could.

And God said, Let us make man in Our own image, after Our likeness: and let them have dominion over the fish of the sea, and over the fowl of the air, and over the cattle, and over all the earth, and over every creeping thing that creepeth upon the earth.

Genesis 1:26

Finally, let us cultivate a spirit of racial pride. Let us learn to be as proud of our race as the Frenchman, German, the Japanese, or the Italian is of his. The race that has faith and pride in itself will eventually win the respect, the confidence and cooperation of the rest of the world.

Now faith is the substance of things hoped for, the evidence of things not seen.

Hebrews 11:1

I will allow no man to drag me down so low as to make me hate him. No race can hate another without itself being narrowed and hated.

Blessed are the pure in heart, for they shall see God.

Matthew 5:8

Racial battles are to be won by marching forward, not by holding back.

Brethren, I count not myself to have apprehended: but this one thing I do, forgetting those things which are behind, and reaching forth unto those things which are before, I press toward the mark for the prize of the high calling of God in Christ Jesus.

Philippians 3:13-14

I have found, too, that it is the visible, the tangible, that goes a long way in softening prejudices. The actual sight of a first-class house that a Negro has built is ten times more potent than pages of discussion about a house that he ought to build, or perhaps could build.

In all labor there is profit, but mere talk leads only to poverty.

Proverbs 14:23

The world may pity a crying, whining race, but it seldom respects it.

For by thy words thou shalt be justified, and by thy words thou shalt be condemned.

Matthew 12:37

There is a certain class of race problem solvers who don't want the patient to get well because as long as the disease holds out, they have not only an easy means of making a living but also an easy medium through which to make themselves prominent before the public.

> *But do not do what they do, for they do not practice what they preach. They tie up heavy loads and put them on men's shoulders, but they themselves are not willing to lift a finger to move them. Everything they do is done for men to see.*
>
> *Matthew 23:3-5*

There are two ways of exerting one's strength; one is pushing down, the other is pulling up.

> *But they that wait upon the Lord shall renew their strength; they shall mount up with wings as eagles; they shall run, and not be weary; and they shall walk, and not faint.*
>
> *Isaiah 40:31*

We shall make a fatal error if we yield to the temptation of believing that mere opposition to our wrongs, and the simple utterance of complaint, will take the place of progressive, constructive action, which must constitute the bedrock of all true civilization.

Here is my servant, whom I uphold, my chosen one in whom I delight; I will put my Spirit on him and he will bring justice to the nations. He will not shout or cry out, or raise his voice in the streets. A bruised reed he will not break, and a smoldering wick he will not snuff out. In faithfulness he will bring forth justice; he will not falter or be discouraged till he establishes justice on earth. In his law the islands will put their hope.

Isaiah 42:1-4

Freedom, in the broadest and highest sense, has never been a bequest; it has been a conquest.

If the Son, therefore shall make you free, ye shall be free indeed.

John 8:36

All the Negro race asks is that the door that rewards industry, thrift, intelligence, and character be left as wide open for him as for the foreigner who constantly comes to our country.

Ask and it will be given to you; seek and you will find; knock and the door will be opened to you. For everyone who asks receives; he who seeks finds; and to him who knocks, the door will be opened.

Matthew 7:7-8

Our republic is the outgrowth of the desire for liberty that is natural in every human breast; freedom of body, mind, and soul, and the most complete guarantee of the safety of life and property.

But whoso looketh into the perfect law of liberty, and continueth therein, he being not a forgetful hearer, but a doer of the work, this man shall be blessed in his deed.

James 1:25

From Tribulation to Triumph

Those who came before us, from Frederick Douglass and Harriet Tubman to Rosa Parks and Martin Luther King, Jr., certainly faced trials that we cannot even imagine so that we would have the advantages that we have today.

Our ancestors worked hard through tribulations because they wanted better for us. As a result, we've gone from sitting on the back of the bus, drinking from separate water fountains, using separate restroom facilities, and not being allowed in certain public places, to running major metropolitan transit systems, and owning and operating multimillion-dollar restaurant chains, movie theatres, and resort hotels. Today there are more blacks in powerful positions than ever before, i.e., judges, police and fire chiefs, and heads of hospitals, corporations, cities, and school districts.

When we make blanket assumptions and statements about an entire race of people still holding us back, we strip ourselves of our own power and we dishonor the work of our ancestors. In celebration of the lives they lived, let's instill in our children their legacies and our achievements so that more and more of them begin making choices from a point of strength, not weakness.

Let us honor our ancestors by recognizing that in an imperfect world, we are still much better off today than when they lived. While there still is some disparity in opportunity, we can take advantage of the many opportunities that they made possible so that we can continue to contribute to the unfolding of a better nation.

From tribulations we grow, we gain experience, and we become wise. It is ultimately from here that we can improve ourselves, we can help to improve our surroundings, and we can encourage and inspire others. It is from here that we, like our ancestors, become triumphant.

Sarah

I have better understanding and deeper insight than all my teachers, because Your testimonies are my meditation.

Psalm 119:99

From Tribulation to Triumph

Quotations from Booker T. Washington

Let us keep before us the fact that, almost without exception, every race or nation that has ever got upon its feet has done so through struggle and trial and persecution; and that out of this very resistance to wrong, out of the struggle against odds, they have gained strength, self-confidence, and experience which they could not have gained in any other way.

> *These things I have spoken to you, that in Me you may have peace. In the world you will have tribulation; but be of good cheer, I have overcome the world.*
>
> *John 16:33*

It is good to be permitted to live in an age when great, serious, and perplexing problems are to be met and solved. For my part I would not care to live in an age when there was no weak part of the human family to be helped up and no wrongs to be righted. Through these means are great men and races produced.

> *Verily, verily, I say unto you, except a corn of wheat fall into the ground and die, it abideth alone: but if it die, it bringeth forth much fruit.*
>
> *John 12:24*

You shall find that by every effort you make to overcome difficulties you are growing in strength and confidence.

Weeping may endure for a night, but joy comes in the morning.

Psalm 30:5

Progress must be the result of severe and constant struggle rather than artificial forcing.

I can do all things through Christ who strengthens me.

Philippians 4:13

I believe every effort we are obliged to make to overcome obstacles will give us strength.

God is our refuge and strength, a very present help in trouble.

Psalm 46:1

There are definite rewards coming to an individual or the race that overcomes obstacles and succeeds in spite of seemingly insurmountable difficulties. The palms of victory are not for the race that merely complains and frets and rails.

Blessed is the man who perseveres under trial, because when he has stood the test, he will receive the crown of life that God has promised to those who love Him.

James 1:12

It is only through struggle and surmounting of difficulties that races, like individuals, are made strong, powerful, and useful.

Many are the afflictions of the righteous; but the Lord delivers him out of them all.

Psalm 34:19

No person can enter industrial life (business) without for a time feeling some days of almost complete failure, but mistakes and weariness beget confidence and experiences.

Cast not away therefore your confidence, which hath great recompense of reward.

Hebrews 10:35

I was never prouder than I am today of being a Negro and of being identified in some slight degree with the struggles and triumphs of a race in which I have such confidence.

Being confident of this very thing, that He which hath begun a good work in you will perform it until the day of Jesus Christ.

Philippians 1:6

No race ever got upon its feet without a struggle, without trials and discouragement.

For a just man falleth seven times, and riseth up again.

Proverbs 24:16

The world needs men, be they black or white, who can rise on successive failures.

The steps of a good man are ordered by the Lord: and he delighteth in his way. Though he fall, he shall not be utterly cast down: for the Lord upholdeth him with His hand.

Psalm 37:23-24

Every race must show to the world by tangible, visible, indisputable evidence that it can do more than merely call attention to the wrong inflicted upon it. The reward of life is for those who choose the good where evil calls out on every hand. That reward is moral character. The more difficult the struggle, the more robust the character.

When a man's ways please the Lord, He makes even his enemies to be at peace with him.

Proverbs 16:7

We must learn to realize that out of contact with difficulties we get a strength and confidence which we can secure in no other manner.

But He knows the way that I take; when He has tested me, I shall come forth as gold.

Job 23:10

Successful Living

A Tribute to My Mother, Gloria Washington Jackson Baskin

I reflect on how many people call her friend; about how rare it is for one to be liked, admired, and respected by so many. I think of her grace, her elegance, and her adaptability. I think about her strength, a strength I know that even she does not realize she possesses.

I reflect on her unwavering commitment and dedication to her family; about how effortlessly she multitasked before it was a "term du jour." She along with her husband raised five children. She worked in the home and she worked outside of the home. Somehow she prepared hot, balanced meals for her family every day. She walked her children to the library every week to ensure that they would love learning. She camped out in the wilderness, when she probably would have preferred to stay in a nice clean hotel. But in doing so, she ensured that her children would learn to love the outdoors and nature. Today, one of her grown sons loves the ocean and the other loves the mountains and the parks.

I reflect on the fact that she was the first black PTA president at her children's elementary school, and on how involved she was with her children and their school. I even think about how naïve she could be at times. When one Easter her children asked for rabbits and chickens, and even a goat, she bought them and brought them home to her nice residential neighborhood. Of course, it wasn't too long before the neighbors insisted that the goat be carted off to a farm.

While nurturing her children, she also rose to the occasion, in uncharted waters for her, to support the career of her husband. I think of the elegant dinner parties when I know she often felt "out of her element," but one would never know it. And when her husband became ill, I remember how unwaveringly she cared for him. He was in and out of the hospital on more occasions than I can remember, but his request was always that she be by his side. The hospital staff rolled in a cot and she would transform the hospital room into "home" until he was well enough to return home. She repeated this loving act over and over again until he passed away, now more than twenty years ago.

I reflect on the times in which life has caused her to stare straight into the face of disappointment and discouragement, and yet she still was able to emerge from these occasions with her joy and her optimism intact. And yes, I even think about her weaknesses and her faults. But what I think about them is how she refuses to yield to them. Sometimes, as we all do, she has to battle, but she never surrenders to defeat. As I watch her grow older, I admire, so much, how she accepts growing older with grace and how unpretentious she is.

She has been blessed with a second husband, Joseph, and she is grandmother to James, Ayyub, Mustafa, Yusuf, Maryam, Lani, Keko, and Evan.

She and my dad are my heroes, and most of what is good about me is because of them. She is my role model. She is the epitome of the definition of a lady, and hers is one of the best examples that I am intimately acquainted with of a successful life. I am blessed to call her Mom.

Gloria

affectionately known to friends and family as "Bonnie"

She openeth her mouth with wisdom: and in her tongue is the law of kindness. She looketh well to the ways of her household, and eateth not the bread of idleness. Her children arise up, and call her blessed: her husband also, and he praiseth her. Many daughters have done virtuously, but thou excellest them all. Favour is deceitful, and beauty is vain: but a woman that feareth the Lord, she shall be praised. Give her of the fruit of her hands; and let her own works praise her in the gates.

Proverbs 31:26-31

Successful Living

Quotations from Booker T. Washington

I have learned that success is to be measured not so much by the position that one has reached in life, as by the obstacles which he has overcome while trying to succeed.

For whatever is born of God overcomes the world. And this is the victory that has overcome the world—our faith.

I John 5:4

A man's position in life is not measured by the heights which he has attained, but by the depths from which he has come.

Then the man said, "Your name will no longer be Jacob, but Israel, because you have struggled with God and with men and have overcome."

Genesis 32:28

The greatness of a nation in the future will be measured not by the vessels that it floats, but by the number of schools and churches and useful industries that it keeps in existence. It will be measured not by the number of men killed, but by the number of men saved and lifted up.

And I, if I be lifted up from the earth, will draw all men unto me.

John 12:32

In seeking after what he terms the ideal, the Negro should not neglect to prepare himself to take advantage of the opportunities that are right about his door.

> *While we look not at the things which are seen, but at the things which are not seen: for the things which are seen are temporal; but the things which are not seen are eternal.*
>
> *II Corinthians 4:18*

We should not permit our grievances to overshadow our opportunity.

> *I will lift up mine eyes unto the hills, from whence cometh my help. My help cometh from the Lord.*
>
> *Psalm 121:1-2*

The first requisite for making life effective for one's self or society is a sound body.

> *What? Know ye not that your body is the temple of the Holy Ghost which is in you, which ye have of God, and ye are not your own? For ye are bought with a price: therefore glorify God in your body, and in your spirit, which are God's.*
>
> *I Corinthians 6:19-20*

Everyone's life is measured by the power that that individual has to make the world better—that is all life is.

For I was hungry and you gave me something to eat, I was thirsty and you gave me something to drink, I was a stranger and you invited me in, I needed clothes and you clothed me, I was sick and you looked after me, I was in prison and you came to visit me.

Matthew 25:35-36

No matter how cheap an article is, it is not a bargain unless you have use for it.

So if you have not been trustworthy in handling worldly wealth, who will trust you with true riches.

Luke 16:11

So long as the Negro is permitted to get an education, acquire property, and secure employment, and is treated with respect in the business or commercial world, I shall have the greatest faith in his working out his own destiny in our Southern states.

And let us not grow weary while doing good, for in due season we shall reap if we do not lose heart.

Galatians 6:9

The greatest thing you can learn is the lesson of brotherly love, usefulness, and of charity.

> *And be ye kind one to another, tenderhearted, forgiving one another, even as God for Christ's sake hath forgiven you.*
>
> *Ephesians 4:32*

The virtues of foresight and thrift and frugality, brought bravely to the front, will bring large material possessions which if properly used will refine and enrich life.

> *But as it is written: "Eye has not seen, nor ear heard, nor have entered into the heart of man the things which God has prepared for those who love Him".*
>
> *1 Corinthians 2:9*

The average man usually has the idea that if he were just somewhere else, in another state or city, or in contact with another race, he would succeed, forgetting too often to utilize the forces that are about him and in hand.

> *The LORD will open to you His good treasures, the heavens, to give rain to your land in its season, and to bless all the work of your hand. You shall lend to many nations, but you shall not borrow. And the LORD will make you the head and not the tail; you shall be above only, and not be beneath, if you heed the commandments of the LORD your God, which I command you today, and are careful to observe them.*
>
> *Deuteronomy 28:12-13*

The future is built on the materials of the past.

How great are His signs, how mighty His wonders! His kingdom is an eternal kingdom; His dominion endures from generation to generation.

Daniel 4:3

In order to be successful in any kind of undertaking one should grow to the point where he completely forgets himself; that is, to lose himself in a great cause.

The man who loves his life will lose it, while the man who hates his life in this world will keep it for eternal life. Whoever serves me must follow me; and where I am, my servant also will be. My Father will honor the one who serves me.

John 12:25-26

I should say that the thing that the colored people of this country need most at this time is solidarity. We need as a race to learn to pull together. There are ten million Negroes in this country. We are a nation within a nation. There is within this ten million individuals a vast latent power, a power which can be awakened only by united action—united action along business, along education, and along religious lines.

Behold, how good and how pleasant it is for brothers to dwell together in unity!

Psalm 133:1

A race of people is a success just in proportion as that race is able to plan today for a hundred years to come.

Then the Lord answered me and said: "Write the vision and make it plain on tablets, that he may run who reads it. For the vision is yet for an appointed time; but at the end it will speak, and it will not lie. Though it tarries, wait for it; because it will surely come, it will not tarry."

Habakkuk 2:2-3

I have never had much patience with the multitudes of people who are always ready to explain why one cannot succeed. I have always had high regard for the man who could tell me how to succeed.

For God hath not given us the spirit of fear; but of power, and of love, and of a sound mind.

II Timothy 1:7

No individual can long succeed unless he keeps in mind the important elements of cleanliness, promptness, system, honesty, and progressiveness.

Since we have these promises, dear friends, let us purify ourselves from everything that contaminates body and spirit, perfecting holiness out of reverence for God.

II Corinthians 7:1

I was born in the South, I have lived and labored in the South, and I expect to die and be buried in the South.

> *The Lord will grant that the enemies who rise up against you will be defeated before you. They will come at you from one direction but flee from you in seven. The Lord will send a blessing on your barns and on everything you put your hand to. The Lord your God will bless you in the land He is giving you.*
>
> *Deuteronomy 28:7-8*

The fellow who is always considering his own selfish interests is not the man who succeeds. The man who is trying to love the higher life in all lines is the individual who will not only succeed here, but also will succeed after he leaves school. In the classroom and elsewhere that individual who sees all that he can do finally succeeds.

> *That your faith should not stand in the wisdom of men, but in the power of God.*
>
> *I Corinthians 2:5*

Success will finally come, by your learning to exercise that patience, self-control, and courage which will make us begin at the bottom and lay the foundation of our growth in the ownership and skillful cultivation of the soil, the possession of a bank account, the exercise of thrift and skill, and the application of the highest culture of hand, head, and heart to the things which the times need have done.

> *My brethren, count it all joy when ye fall into divers temptations; Knowing this, that the trying of your faith worketh patience. But let patience have her perfect work, that ye may be perfect and entire, wanting nothing.*
>
> *James 1:2-4*

As I now look back over my life, I do not recall that I ever became discouraged over anything I set out to accomplish.

> *I have glorified thee on the earth: I have finished the work which thou gavest me to do*
>
> *John 17:4*

The Dignity and The Beauty of Labor

A Tribute to My Mother, Agnes Louise Washington O'Neal

As long as I can remember, my mother exemplified the dignity of labor as she followed in the footsteps of her grandfather Booker T. Washington. She worked diligently just as she always vowed she would, until the day she died, a little over three months shy of her eightieth birthday.

At seventeen years old my mother left her birthplace of Tuskegee, Alabama, for Tennessee State University, where in 1940 she completed her degree in the field of business. She applied her education continuously as she expertly improved the efficiency of each organization she worked in.

She never made a lot of money, but that never deterred her from doing an exceptional job. As a single mother it was difficult for her to raise my brother James and me, but even that did not deter her from doing outstanding work. She performed above her job duties, more than earned her pay, and with what she made she managed to keep a roof over our heads. For a long time while I was growing up, she worked two full-time jobs.

After the big earthquake here in the San Francisco Bay Area in 1989, which occurred just two weeks before her seventieth birthday, she received a letter from the president of the company she worked for, stating, "I want to thank you for the professionalism you displayed during and after the recent earthquake.... Your composure and actions were the principle factor for settling the concerns and panic that some residents exhibited...."

I remember being terrified myself after that event, and at the same time I was worried sick about my mother. With no lights all over the city of Oakland, and people waiting in long lines to get gas, it was several hours before I finally made it across town to be with her. To my surprise, what I found was my mother, a calm soul, with a flashlight in her hands, diligently working to see that everyone in the building where she worked was safe and sound.

In her lifetime she created a mark of excellence by holding several impressive positions, including working in Washington, D.C., simultaneously for Howard Thurman during the day and Mary McCloud Bethune in the evening. Also in Washington, D.C., she was the first black to work for the Department of Agriculture, and she worked for a period of time on the campus of Tuskegee Institute at the airbase among the famous Tuskegee Airmen.

After working diligently and tenaciously all her adult life and never complaining about her work, today she peacefully rests in the family cemetery, on the grounds of Tuskegee University, among two of the most distinguished laborers of our time, her grandfather Booker T. Washington and George Washington Carver. I believe this is a sign of her eternal blessings for the work she did here on earth.

We can greatly benefit from the model of ethics that my mother demonstrated in the workforce. If our dreams are important, whatever they may be, we will come closer to realizing them if we make up our minds to do the very best we can in whatever task we set out to do until we reach them.

Sarah

All things work together for good to them that love God, to them who are the called according to his purpose.

Romans 8:28

The Dignity and The Beauty of Labor

Quotations from Booker T. Washington

There is little hope in this world for any people until the people of this world have learned the disgrace of idleness and the dignity and beauty of all kinds of labor.

> *Laziness brings a deep sleep, and the shiftless man goes hungry.*
>
> *Proverbs 19:15*

I believe that when one can grow to the point where he loves his work, this gives him a kind of strength that is most valuable.

> *Moreover, when God gives any man wealth and possessions, and enables him to enjoy them, to accept his lot and be happy in his work—this is a gift of God.*
>
> *Ecclesiastes 5:19*

One should make it a rule never to let his work drive him, but to so master it, and keep it in such complete control, and to keep so far ahead of it, that he will be the master instead of the servant.

> *Therefore, my dear brothers, stand firm. Let nothing move you. Always give yourselves fully to the work of the Lord, because you know that your labor in the Lord is not in vain.*
>
> *I Corinthians 15:58*

Our harvest is always in proportion to the amount of earnest labour that we put into our work

> *Do you see a man diligent and skillful in his business? He will stand before kings; he will not stand before obscure men.*
>
> *Proverbs 22:29*

If in the providence of God the Negro got any good out of slavery, he got the habit of work.

> *But as for you, ye thought evil against me; but God meant it unto good.*
>
> *Genesis 50:20*

There is a physical and mental enjoyment that comes from the consciousness of being the absolute master of one's work in all its details, that is very satisfactory and inspiring. If one learns to follow this plan, he gets a freshness of body and vigor of mind out of work that goes a long way toward keeping him strong and healthy.

Blessed are all who fear the Lord, who walk in His ways. You will eat the fruit of your labor; blessings and prosperity will be yours.

Psalm 128:1-2

We get out of every venture just what we put into it; no more, no less. To attain success we must put forth hard and honest labour.

He who gathers crops in summer is a wise son, but he who sleeps during harvest is a disgraceful son.

Proverbs 10:5

When any people, regardless of race or geographical location, have not been trained to habits of industry, have not been given skill of hand in youth and taught to love labor, a direct result is the breeding of a worthless, idle class, which spends a great deal of its time in trying to live by its wits.

For even when we were with you, this we commanded you, that if any would not work, neither should he eat. For we hear that there are some which walk among you disorderly, working not at all, but are busybodies.

II Thessalonians 3:10-11

We must not only become reliable, progressive, skillful, and intelligent, but we must keep the idea constantly before our youths that all forms of labor, whether with the hand or head, are honorable.

Train up a child in the way he should go, and when he is old he will not depart from it.

Proverbs 22:6

The opportunity to earn a dollar in a factory just now is worth infinitely more than the opportunity to spend a dollar in an opera house.

He has filled them with skill to do all kinds of work as craftsman, designers, embroiderers in blue, purple and scarlet yarn and fine linen, and weavers——all of them master craftsmen and designers.

Exodus 35:35

No race can prosper till it learns that there is as much dignity in tilling a field as in writing a poem.

Remember to extol His work, which men have praised in song. All mankind has seen it; men gaze on it from afar.

Job 36:24-25

Nothing ever comes to one, that is worth having, except as a result of hard work.

From the fruit of his words a man shall be satisfied with good, and the work of a man's hands shall come back to him (as a harvest).

Proverbs 12:14

Economic Development

I often wonder how economically strong our race would be today had we continued to follow the guidance of Booker T. Washington regarding the paramount necessity and priority of economic development and land acquisition. It is my belief that had we stayed consistent to the course he charted over one hundred years ago, we would now be owners in far greater numbers than we are consumers.

The concept of an ownership society is not a new one in the black community. Long before the establishment of the National Urban League, black economic-development corporations, black chambers of commerce, and the various black business associations that today are in operation around the nation, Booker T. Washington spearheaded a group of black businessmen and formed the National Negro Business League.

Among the League's members were A. G. Gaston, said to be the wealthiest black man in America when he died at age 104 in 1996, and Phillip Payton, a wealthy realtor and the developer of large areas of Harlem. Madame C. J. Walker, the first known American female self-made millionaire, who happened to be black, was also a member. They were all zealous adherents to Booker T. Washington's economic philosophy—that blacks would never truly be liberated until they could compete economically in America and in the world, and that ownership of real property, which often brings material wealth, is critical to the progress of our race.

Shortly before he died, Booker T. Washington expressed that he was most proud of the fact that by 1910 roughly 2,500,000 black Americans were living in homes that they owned, that black farmers owned and operated more than a billion dollars worth of cultivated farms, and that black businesses were thriving throughout the country. As cited in the publication *Christian Business Legends*, by the year 1905, Tuskegee had produced more self-made millionaires than Yale, Harvard, and Princeton combined.

Just as Booker T. Washington used his considerable blessings to bless others, it is our moral responsibility, as we are blessed, to reach out to be a blessing to those who are less fortunate.

Gloria

Call unto me, and I will answer thee, and show thee great and mighty things, which thou knowest not.

Jeremiah 33:3

Economic Development

Quotations from Booker T. Washington

There are certain great natural and economic laws that govern the problems of nations and races. Soil, rain, and sunshine draw no color line. The forces of nature will yield their wealth as quickly to the hands of the brown man, the yellow man, as they will to the hands of any other race. Man may discriminate, but the economic laws of trade and commerce cannot discriminate.

> *Where were you when I laid the earth's foundation? Have you ever given orders to the morning, or shown the dawn its place, that it might take the earth by the edges and shake the wicked out of it?*
>
> *Job 38:4, 12-13*

The individual who can do something that the world wants done will, in the end, make his way regardless of his race.

> *For I know the plans I have for you, declares the Lord, plans to prosper you and not to harm you, plans to give you hope and a future.*
>
> *Jeremiah 29:11*

I would put as a condition of success in life, whether it relates to the individual or the race, ownership in the soil, cleaving to mother earth.

She considers a field and buys it; from her profits she plants a vineyard.

Proverbs 31:16

No individual should feel satisfied until he has a comfortable home.

But as for me and my house, we will serve the Lord.

Joshua 24:15

Economic independence is the foundation of political independence. We must act in these matters before others from foreign lands rob us of our birthright. Land ownership is the foundation of all wealth.

Believe on the Lord your God, so shall ye be established; believe His prophets, so shall ye prosper.

II Chronicles 20:20

The Negro should be taught book learning, yes, but along with it he should be taught that book education and industrial development must go hand in hand. No race which fails to do this can ever hope to succeed.

Blessed is the man who finds wisdom, the man who gains understanding, for she (wisdom) is more profitable than silver and yields better returns than gold.

Proverbs 3:13-14

The individual that owns the property, pays the taxes, possesses the intelligence and substantive character is the one who is going to exercise the greatest control in government, whether he lives in the North or whether he lives in the South.

> *For unto us a Child is born, unto us a Son is given; and the government will be upon His shoulder. And His name will be called Wonderful, Counselor, Mighty God and Everlasting Father, Prince of Peace.*
>
> *Isaiah 9:6*

No race that has anything to sell to the markets of the world is long in any degree ostracized.

> *People curse the man who hoards grain, but blessing crowns him who is willing to sell.*
>
> *Proverbs 11:26*

I do not believe that the world ever takes a race seriously, in its desire to enter into the control of the government of a nation in any large way, until a large number of individuals, members of that race, have demonstrated, beyond question, their ability to control and develop individual business enterprises.

> *And Jesus answering saith unto them, "Have faith in God. For verily I say unto you, that whosoever shall say unto this mountain, be thou removed, and be thou cast into the sea; and shall not doubt in his heart, but shall believe that those things which he saith shall come to pass; he shall have whatsoever he saith."*
>
> *Mark 11:22-23*

Aim to be your own employers as speedily as possible.

She sets about her work vigorously; her arms are strong for her tasks. She sees that her trading is profitable, and her lamp does not go out at night.

Proverbs 31:17-18

The salvation of the black man in the South is his owning the soil he cultivates.

They will build houses and dwell in them; they will plant vineyards and eat their fruit. No longer will they build houses and others live in them, or plant and others eat.

Isaiah 65:21-22

Crime among us decreases as ownership in property increases.

He who works his land will have abundant food, but he who chases fantasies lacks judgment.

Proverbs 12:11

We should never forget that the ownership and cultivation of the soil constitutes the foundation of great wealth and usefulness among our people. A land-less race is like a ship without a rudder.

But thou shalt remember the Lord thy God: for it is He that giveth thee power to get wealth, that He may establish His covenant which He sware unto thy fathers, as it is this day.

Deuteronomy 8:18

We must catch the spirit of modern progress and achievement, or be shut out by those who have.

For everyone who has will be given more, and he will have an abundance. Whoever does not have, even what he has will be taken from him.

Matthew 25:29

The black man that has mortgages on a dozen men's houses will have no trouble in voting and having his vote counted.

Except the Lord build the house, they labour in vain that build it: except the Lord keep the city, the watchman waketh but in vain.

Psalm 127:1

It was natural and right that in the beginning of our freedom the work of the teacher and minister should receive the greatest attention. There is still an emphatic need for more teachers and ministers, but we have now reached, as a race, a new era, almost a crisis, in our growth. Along by the side of the teacher and minister we must have in increasing numbers the independent farmer, the merchant, the banker, and other kinds of business men and woman. These will strengthen the teacher and minister, and they in turn will help the businessman.

But now are they many members, yet but one body. And whether one member suffer, all the members suffer with it; or one member be honoured, all the members rejoice with it. Now ye are the body of Christ, and members in particular.

I Corinthians 12:20, 26-27

More and more thoughtful students of the race problem are beginning to see that business and industry constitute what we may call the strategic points in its solution.

For a dream cometh through the multitude of business; and a fool's voice is known by multitude of words.

Ecclesiastes 5:3

No man who continues to add something to the material intellectual and moral well-being of the place in which he lives is long left without proper reward.

A good man leaves an inheritance to his children's children, but the wealth of the sinner is stored up for the righteous.

Proverbs 13:22

What we should do in all our schools is to turn out fewer job-seekers and more job-makers. Any one can seek a job, but it requires a person of rare ability to create a job.

It is for freedom that Christ has set us free. Stand firm, then, and do not let yourselves be burdened again by a yoke of slavery.

Galatians 5:1

Helpful to Humanity

Today, in what is said to be the best and the worst of times, as a race we are self-destructing in record numbers. In my work with "at-risk" youth and their families, too often I find that this destruction is self-afflicted—going back and moving forward through the generations.

Domestic violence and child abuse; broken homes and fatherless children; alcohol and drug abuse; gang violence and incarceration—all rank high among our afflictions. The result of these afflictions is anger, frustration, and depression. They create turmoil in our homes, which has a domino effect—first destroying our families, and then spilling over into our communities.

In the New Testament we learn that God's greatest command is to love Him with all our heart, all our soul, and our entire mind. His second greatest command guides us to love our neighbor as we love ourselves. Therefore, if we are to effectively love others and help others, we must first learn to properly love and help ourselves.

We must be willing first to look deep inside ourselves, eliminating any self-hatred from our mind, and then take responsibility for our actions. This allows healing to take place from within. We will then have a far greater capacity to spread love to others in a way that is healthy, productive, and long-term. Only then can we begin to bring healing into our homes, and ultimately into our communities. Only then can we truly be helpful to humanity.

Sarah

I will praise thee; for I am fearfully and wonderfully made: marvelous are thy works; and that my soul knoweth right well.

Psalm 139:14

Helpful to Humanity

Quotations from Booker T. Washington

The highest test of the civilization of any race is in its willingness to extend a helping hand to the less fortunate. A race, like an individual, lifts itself up by lifting others up.

> *And the King will answer and say to them, "Assuredly, I say to you, inasmuch as you did it to one of the least of these my brethren, you did it to Me."*
>
> *Matthew 25:40*

I pity the man, black or white, who has never experienced the joy and satisfaction that comes to one by reason of an effort to assist in making someone else more useful and happier.

> *Let each one of us make it a practice to please (make happy) his neighbor for his good and for his true welfare, to edify him [to strengthen him and build him up spiritually].*
>
> *Romans 15:2*

The happiest individuals are those who do the most to make others useful and happy.

A generous man will prosper; he who refreshes others will himself be refreshed.

Proverbs 11:25

The only thing worth living for is the lifting up of our fellow men.

For if they fall, the one will lift up his fellow: but woe to him that is alone when he falleth; for he hath not another to help him up.

Ecclesiastes 4:10

Until we get to the point where we can get happiness and supreme satisfaction out of helping our fellows, we are not truly educated.

It is more blessed to give than to receive.

Acts 20:35

The happiest people in the world are those who do the most for others; the most miserable are those who do the least.

Be not deceived; God is not mocked: for whatsoever a man soweth, that shall he also reap.

Galatians 6:7

A life is not worth much of which it cannot be said, when it comes to its close, that it was helpful to humanity.

This is how we know what love is: Jesus Christ laid down his life for us. And we ought to lay down our lives for our brothers.

1 John 3:16

It is the quiet, unseen giving which never reaches the ear of the world, that makes possible the existence of the best things of the world.

Give, and it will be given to you. A good measure, pressed down, shaken together and running over, will be poured into your lap. For with the measure you use, it will be measured to you.

Luke 6:38

In proportion as one renders service he becomes great.

You, my brothers, were called to be free. But do not use your freedom to indulge the sinful nature; rather, serve one another in love.

Galatians 5:13

He who goes into the battle of life giving a smile for every frown, a cheery word for every cross one, and lending a helping hand to the unfortunate, is after all the best missionary.

Therefore go and make disciples of all nations, baptizing them in the name of the Father and of the Son and of the Holy Spirit, and teaching them to obey everything I have commanded you. And surely I am with you always, to the very end of the age.

Matthew 28:19-20

The more you do to make someone else happy, the more happiness will you receive in return. If you want to be happy, if you want to live a life of genuine pleasure, do something for somebody else.

Do nothing out of selfish ambition or vain conceit, but in humility consider others better than yourselves. Each of you should look not only to your own interests, but also to the interests of others.

Philippians 2:3-4

When you feel unhappy, disagreeable, and miserable go to someone else who is miserable and do that person an act of kindness and you will find that you will be made happy.

Bear one another's burdens, and thereby fulfill the law of Christ.

Galatians 6:2

Lay hold of something that will help you, and then use it to help somebody else.

In the same way, faith by itself, if it is not accompanied by action, is dead.

James 2:17

In the final test, the success of our race will be in proportion to the service that it renders to the world. In the long run the badge of service is the badge of sovereignty.

The greatest among you will be your servant. For whoever exalts himself will be humbled, and whoever humbles himself will be exalted.

Matthew 23:11-12

Growing in His Image

As we begin our journey with God, we must enter into and establish a relationship with Him. He is the one who created us and who knows us perfectly, and yet loves us unconditionally. While others may disappoint us and let us down, God is always with us and He always remains the same.

As we grow in our relationship with Him, we learn to let go, to yield, and to allow Him through the Spirit within us to take the reigns of the life that He gave us as a gift. He is like a potter and He patiently works with us like a piece of clay as He molds us and shapes us into a better self.

As we grow from spiritual infancy to greater and greater spiritual maturity we learn to trust God and to walk by faith. We learn that our time, our talents, our gifts, our opportunities, and our potentialities are all gifts from God over which He has simply made us managers. We willingly begin to give those very gifts back to Him to be used in service for His plan and His purpose for our life.

As we grow we begin to seek God with our whole heart by studying and meditating on His Word until it actually becomes a part of us. Eventually we acquire a renewed mind and a transformed heart. It becomes our delight to demonstrate our love for God through praise and worship and through obedience to His Word. We learn to let go of our pride and to ask for forgiveness and to forgive others. We even learn to love those who seem to be unlovable.

Growing in His image means honoring our mothers and our fathers and loving our neighbors as we love ourselves. It also means that we begin to tell others about this wonderful relationship. Our prayer becomes that our lives will draw others to God as they witness the change that God has made in us. It means we become ministers of reconciliation and ambassadors for Christ on the earth; and it ultimately means we become more and more like Him, and we rule and reign with Him forever in His Kingdom.

Gloria

For God so loved the world, that He gave His only begotten son, that whoever believes in Him shall not perish, but have eternal life.

John 3:16

Growing in His Image

Quotations from Booker T. Washington

No man's life is really complete until he owns a Bible that is part of himself. One of the most valuable lessons I ever learned at this institute (Hampton Institute) was the value of the Bible. For the first time in my life I had put into my hands a copy of that book which I could call my own. And ever since, I have possessed that Bible. No matter how busy I may be and no matter how many responsibilities crowd upon me, I never have let a day pass without taking my Bible and reading a chapter or at least a few verses. It is valuable from an historical and literary point of view; it is more valuable from a spiritual point of view.

And ye shall seek me, and find me, when ye shall search for me with all your heart.

Jeremiah 29:13

To be one with God is to be like God. Our real religious striving then should be to become one with God; sharing with Him in our poor humble way His qualities and attributes.

Now the Lord is the Spirit, and where the Spirit of the Lord is, there is freedom. And we, who with unveiled faces all reflect the Lord's glory, are being transformed into His likeness with ever-increasing glory, which comes from the Lord, who is the Spirit.

II Corinthians 3:17-18

Tuskegee shall be thoroughly Christian but strictly undenominational. In a two-year course of study a student will learn not only the Bible, but how to prepare a sermon, how to read a hymn, how to study, and most important, how to reach and help the people outside of the pulpit in an unselfish Christian way, to take the power for good to reach the masses.

> *If ye continue in My word, then are ye My disciples indeed; And ye shall know the truth, and the truth shall make you free.*
>
> *John 8:31-32*

I make it a rule never to go before an audience, on any occasion, without asking the blessing of God upon what I want to say.

> *The effectual fervent prayer of a righteous man availeth much.*
>
> *James 5:16*

Our people will grow in proportion as we teach them that the way to have the most of Jesus, and in permanent form, is to mix with their religion some land, cotton, and corn, a house with two or three rooms, and a little bank account.

> *Therefore you shall keep every commandment which I commanded you today, that you may be strong, and go in and possess the land which you cross over to possess, and that you may prolong your days in the land which the LORD swore to give your fathers, to them and their descendants, 'a land flowing with milk and honey.'*
>
> *Deuteronomy 11:8-9*

The Negro needs not only that religion that is going to fill his heart, but that kind which is going to fill his stomach, clothe and shelter his body, and employ his hands.

Therefore do not worry, saying, what shall we eat? Or what shall we drink? Or what shall we wear? For after all these things the Gentiles seek. For your heavenly Father knows you need all these things. But seek first the kingdom of God and His righteousness and all these things shall be added to you.

Matthew 6:31-33

If no other consideration had convinced me of the value of the Christian life, the Christ-like work of some churches for the elevation of the black man would have made me Christian.

And now abide faith, hope, love, these three; but the greatest of these is love.

1 Corinthians 13:13

As the white man in all parts of America becomes more educated, cultured, and more truly a Christian; in that same proportion will the white man be less willing to withhold justice from the Negro.

Direct my footsteps according to your word, let no sin rule over me.

Psalm 119:133

We went into slavery in this country pagans: we came out Christian.

Therefore, if anyone is in Christ, he is a new creation; old things have passed away; behold, all things have become new.

II Corinthians 5:17

The minister in the Negro church has an influence for good or evil, is looked to for advice on all subjects, to an extent that is not true of any other class of ministers in this country.

For God is not unrighteous to forget your work and labour of love, which ye have shown toward His name, in that ye have ministered to the saints, and do minister.

Hebrews 6:10

If we imitate the life of Christ as nearly as possible, heaven will come about more and more here on this earth.

Thy kingdom come. Thy will be done in earth, as it is in heaven.

Matthew 6:10

Our people need to be taught that it is better to be a Christian than to be a Methodist or a Baptist, that it is better to save a soul than subscribe to a creed.

Thus have ye made the commandment of God of none effect by your tradition.

Matthew 15:6

Sentimental Christianity, which banks everything in the future and nothing in the present, is the curse of the race.

And Jesus answered and said, "Verily I say unto you, there is no man that hath left house, or brethren, or sisters, or father, or mother, or wife, or children, or lands, for my sake, and the gospel's, but he shall receive an hundredfold, now in this time, houses, brethren, and sisters, and mothers, and children, and lands, with persecutions; and in the world to come eternal life."

Mark 10:29-30

There are persons whose lives are so much like that of Christ's, who have so much genuine Christianity in them, that we cannot come into contact with them, we cannot even steal a glance at their faces, without being made stronger and better.

Arise, shine; for thy light is come, and the glory of the Lord is risen upon thee.

Isaiah 60:1

If there is any good in a person, let us seek to find it; the evil will take care of itself.

The good man brings good things out of the good stored up in him, and the evil man brings evil things out of the evil stored up in him. But I tell you that men will have to give account on the day of judgment for every careless word they have spoken. For by your words you will be acquitted, and by your words you will be condemned.

Matthew 12:35-37

Great men cultivate love, and only little men cherish the spirit of hatred.

But the fruit of the Spirit is love, joy, peace, longsuffering, kindness, goodness, faithfulness, gentleness, self-control. Against such there is no law.

Galatians 5:22-23

A man is free just in proportion as he learns to live within God's law, and he makes grievous mistakes and serious blunders the moment he departs from these laws.

This book of the law shall not depart out of thy mouth; but thou shalt meditate therein day and night, that thou mayest observe to do according to all that is written therein: for then thou shalt make thy way prosperous, and then thou shalt have good success.

Joshua 1:8

Our religion must not alone be the concern of the emotions, but must be woven into the warp and woof of our everyday life.

But be ye doers of the word, and not hearers only, deceiving your own selves.

James 1:22

Each of you, in beginning your school year, should have a Bible, and you should make that Bible a part of your school life, a part of your very nature, and always, no matter how busy the day may be, no matter how many mistakes, no matter how many failures you make in other directions, do not fail to find a few minutes to study or read your Bible.

In the beginning was the Word, and the Word was with God, and the Word was God. And the Word was made flesh, and dwelt among us, (and we beheld His glory, the glory as of the only begotten of the Father), full of grace and truth.

John 1:1, 14

The greatest people in the world, those who are most learned, those who bear the burdens and responsibilities of the world, are persons who are not ashamed to let the world know not only that they believe in the Bible, but that they read it.

For I am not ashamed of the gospel of Christ: for it is the power of God unto salvation to every one that believeth; to the Jew first, and also to the Greek. For therein is the righteousness of God revealed from faith to faith: as it is written, the just shall live by faith.

Romans 1:16-17

I believe that every day is a judgment that we reap our rewards daily and that wherever we sin, we are punished by mental and physical anxiety and by a weakened character that separates us from God. Every day is, I take it, a day of judgment, and as we learn God's laws and grow into His likeness we shall find ourselves, in this world, a life of usefulness and honor.

If we confess our sins, He is faithful and just to forgive us our sins and to cleanse us from all unrighteousness.

I John 1:9

Epilogue

A Personal Testimony from Gloria Yvonne Jackson

My earliest recollection of my great-grandfather is that of my parents sharing with me the majestic legacy that I, and all of those in our family, carried as a result of having been born in the direct bloodline of Booker T. Washington. They frequently reminded me that it was a legacy of which I could be proud and one I had an obligation to share with others.

But it was only a few years ago, after stumbling across an old publication that carried the newspaper accounts, from both the black press and the white press, of Booker T. Washington's death, that the truth of my parents' words, of the majesty of this man, came alive in my heart. I always knew that he was a remarkable man; however, the respect with which people from all over world regarded him at that time served to impress upon my heart just how widely regarded and how appreciated my great-grandfather was.

During his lifetime, throngs of people would line up along the railroad tracks anticipating his visit to their town or city and thousands would come out to hear him speak. People from every race and every social stratum and even those who disagreed with my great-grandfather deeply respected him.

As I was pouring over the newspaper accounts of his death, over the remembrances, the condolences, and over the memorial program held in his honor, I actually found myself feeling a very deep sense of sadness. As I reflected on the emotion I was experiencing, I realized that it was not sadness directed at the death of my great-grandfather, as he had passed away so many years before; rather, it was sadness over the loss to a whole generation of his truthful and honorable legacy.

So few people today fully realize or acknowledge his extraordinary contribution toward laying the foundation for our race as we began the very difficult walk up from slavery to freedom. It seems even fewer people appreciate the considerable advances achieved by our race under his leadership, in the very short time since slavery had been abolished.

Booker T. Washington understood, and successfully conveyed to others, that freedom is not simply the physical freedom that had been secured by the culmination of the Civil War but that true freedom is as much an internal process as it is an external one. It is as much, if not more, about the condition of one's mind as it is about the condition of one's body. It is a right given by God that carries with it an awesome responsibility.

He understood that true liberty necessitated the ability to care for oneself and one's family and that it required the foundation of a strong and stable economic base and economic independence. Tuskegee Normal and Industrial Institute (now University) was appropriately founded on July 4, 1881—Independence Day. Tuskegee is where so many of the masses of poor blacks, recently emancipated from physical slavery, had the opportunity to receive an education and to learn skills that would assist them to become fully free. It was for this freedom that Booker T. Washington poured out his life.

Sadly, it was my generation that was in large measure responsible for minimizing, and in some cases even vilifying, Booker T. Washington and his achievements. After the moral and righteous civil rights victories that were won under the wise leadership of the Rev. Dr. Martin Luther King, Jr., some in my generation began to de-emphasize the very principles that had been so instrumental in securing those victories, and the principles that had sustained us up to that point. Over time a subtle shift in attitude began to take root. The focus for some was no longer on the principle that with equal opportunity and equal access we would achieve just as any other group achieves, but rather on looking to sources outside ourselves for racial advance.

Booker T. Washington, whose philosophy for the uplift of our race centered on education, hard work, economic independence, and personal responsibility, was increasingly portrayed in a negative light. In many circles his voice was eventually silenced and his message of self-reliance was blocked.

Fortunately, there were also those of my generation and beyond who were and who remain deeply impressed and influenced by Booker T. Washington's hopeful and empowering philosophy. Many in previous generations aggressively applied his uplifting philosophy to their lives.

I cannot think of a more inspiring example of one who successfully applied the philosophy of Booker T. Washington to his life than my dad. Though born into poverty, neither he nor his parents allowed poverty to become a part of their spirit. By utilizing the resources immediately at hand, which included the church, the YMCA, and the library, and by applying the principles of hard work, accountability, discipline, and excellence, he achieved beyond most expectations, as did many of his friends. He was rewarded for his efforts when, among many honors, he became the first black American surgeon to be named to the staff of the prestigious Cedars-Sinai Hospital in Los Angeles, California.

Over 9,000 people poured into the little town of Tuskegee to honor my great-grandfather on the occasion of the memorial service paying tribute to his life. They came from all over the world—all manner of people, including noblemen, dignitaries, and businesspeople. I have photographs of the simple people from the countryside who by the hundreds walked for miles on that chilly November day just to say thank you and to pay their respects to this man who so loved his race and who had such confidence in his race. They were determined to honor Booker T. Washington who, with God's help, had done everything in his power to advance his people. Those who were unable to attend weighed in with cards, letters, flowers, and with gifts. To demonstrate the widespread respect with which he was held and the enormity of the occasion, businesses were closed and flags were flown at half-staff. I believe a seed had been sown.

Not too long ago, somewhere I read the words "Booker rising." I like the way that sounds. It implies that with all that has been done to stifle and to diminish the message and the true accomplishments of Booker T. Washington, his truth and his legacy are on the rise. We are informed that though there may be a crucifixion, there is always a resurrection where truth is involved. Could it be that on the occasion of the 150th year since his birth, it is now a time of harvest?

I am grateful and I am honored that God has blessed me through my heritage, through public speaking and writing, and through my organization, the Booker T. Washington Inspirational Network, Inc., to be instrumental in some small measure in placing the truth of the legacy of my great-grandfather back into the public domain.

Booker T. Washington was characterized by those making presentations at the memorial service honoring him, and in the newspaper accounts of his death, in the following way: He was one who had the courage to launch out into the deep at the command of his savior; one who walked on the water when Jesus called; and one who, like Moses, endured as seeing Him who is invisible. I am humbled to be a member of the family of this remarkable leader.

I join with my cousin Sarah in proclaiming, "To God be all the glory."

Gloria Yvonne Jackson

Final Thoughts

Booker T. Washington was a practical man of far reaching vision. In addition to Tuskegee Institute, which spawned so many other schools and universities, and so many of what today we call the historically black colleges, Booker T. Washington founded and established a teachers' institute, a ministers' night school, a hospital, a rural school improvement campaign, a community beautification project, a weekly farm paper, a circulating library, and a farming community for agricultural graduates of Tuskegee. He also developed a systematic program to improve conditions in jails and chain gangs, and for the rehabilitation of released prisoners.

He sat on the boards of Fisk and Howard universities, and directed philanthropic aid to these and other black colleges and universities. Today, Tuskegee graduates live and work all over the world, demonstrating the strength of Booker T. Washington's philosophy.

He promoted black advancement through undercover and anonymous sponsorship of civil rights lawsuits and as a ghostwriter of editorials in newspapers across the country. For those blacks who were qualified to sit in seats of government, Booker T. Washington used his considerable influence to make certain that occurred. He also used his influence to insure that federal judicial appointments would include judges who would give blacks a fair hearing.

The National Negro Business League founded by Booker T. Washington, birthed, The National Negro Press Association, The National Negro Funeral Directors' Association, The National Negro Bar Association, The National Negro Retail Merchants' Association and The National Association of Negro Insurance Men.

"*He was unselfish and generous to a fault; he was modest yet masterful; he was quiet yet intense; his common sense and sagacity seemed uncanny, such was his knowledge of human nature. His was a great soul in which no bitterness or littleness could even find a lurking place. His was the great heart of Lincoln, with malice toward none and charity for all. He loved all men and all men loved him. My humble prayer is that his torch has lighted another among the dark millions of America, to lead the race onward and upward.*"

(William H. Lewis, Assistant U.S. Attorney General and first black captain of the Harvard University Football Team—1915)

So from an old clay cabin in Virginia's hills, Booker T. Washington rose up to be one of the nation's great leaders. He lit a torch in Alabama, then darkness fled.

Dr. Martin Luther King, Jr.

I have fought a good fight, I have finished my course, I have kept the faith.

II Timothy 4:7

Index of Scriptures

All scriptures taken from the King James, New King James, New International, New American Standard and the Amplified versions of the Holy Bible.

Chapter 2   Exalt Excellence

Chapter 3   Education of The Head, The Hand, and The Heart

Chapter 4   Race Relations — Let Freedom Ring!

Chapter 5 From Tribulation to Triumph

Chapter 6   Successful Living

Chapter 7   The Dignity and The Beauty of Labor

Chapter 8 Economic Development

Chapter 9 Helpful to Humanity

Chapter 10 Growing in His Image

Closing Page

Notes

Notes

Notes

Notes

Notes

Notes

Printed in the United States
72811LV00003B/220-294